AF484045

THE STAR COLLECTOR

HAILEY RENEE

Copyright © 2026 by Stone & Spirit Press

All rights reserved.

No part of this book may be reproduced in any form or by any electronic or mechanical means, including information storage and retrieval systems, without written permission from the author, except for the use of brief quotations in a book review.

No part of this book may be used or reproduced in any manner for the purpose of training artificial intelligence technologies or systems.

Interior design by NassyArt

Cover design by Getcovers

 Formatted with Vellum

*For those learning to begin again,
may you find your fire,
as I have.*

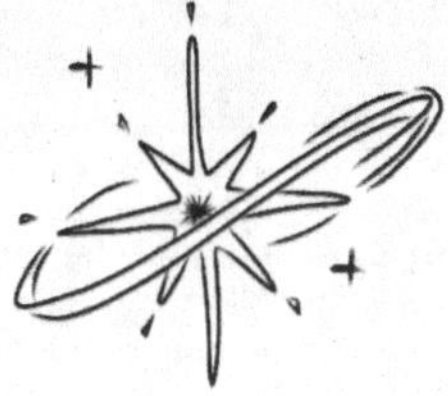

STARDUST

He called tonight.
Not a warning,
just a voice that creaked through the quiet
and pulled the air from my lungs.

And just like that,
the wound I'd buried
remembered how to bleed.

And I gave you light
with the last match I had.
Leaving myself freezing.

Let the thunder know my name,
drown this soft and silent shame.
For what is pain,
if not a prayer,
for someone who
was never there?

I am a shell of the person I was,
scraped thin by survival—
but could I ever be something
if I still belong to you?

I ache over your quiet mouth,
begging for words,
even if they happen to hurt.

Running.
That is my inheritance.
Running, running,
away from you,
away from what you carried
and what you gave me.
I run, but I feel the ache
of what was never fixed,
the grief I didn't choose.
I am still running,
away from you.

I am born of silence,
of hands that never held me,
of voices that taught me
how to fold myself small.

She carried storms in her chest,
unhealed, unbroken, unyielding,
her shadows pressed into my spine,
whispering the curses she could not name.

I walk through this house of old wounds,
tracing the cracks in the walls
where their pain has settled like dust,
and I feel it in my marrow.

I saw the stars tonight,
in a way that broke me,
as if the universe knew
all the things I could not hold.

But tonight,
I only ache,
a hollow in motion,
a shell learning
that the stars
do not heal,
they only remind you
that something more
is always waiting.

This morning,
my arms ache like roots
forced to grow too fast,
strained beneath the weight of silence,
and the burden of staying.
The house feels like a reflection of my insides:
too full, too empty, too still.
I don't want to speak.
I don't want to be known today.

Touch me,
but not like them,
not with hands that claim ownership,
that leave their history
pressed into my skin.
Spare me.

And still,
I call his name,
like it might save me
as I swallow the scream.

My soul is an eclipse,
swallowed by shadows
I cannot shift or name.

I stand in the ashes of my own life.
A childhood burned up too quickly,
a decade of love
spent learning how not to hold on.

Learning to let go is like learning to walk,
you are still looking for a hand,
but the hands you knew
were always too tight, too cold, too gone.

I want to reach,
to be held, to be safe,
but my body remembers
how hands can hurt as much as they heal.

I begged the universe
to wash your name from my mouth,
and learned too late
it had already branded my heart.

Will I ever find my fire?
I whisper to the sun,
tears burning trails
down my red cheeks.
I am so tired of reaching
into empty air,
of mistaking warmth
for something that will stay.
I need something to hold on to,
something that does not disappear
when I loosen my grip,
but nothing holds on to me.

The smoke lingers in my lungs,
ghosts of hands that should have stayed,
voices that never cradled me,
lessons I never wanted to learn.

When I was younger,
I was taught to catch lightning bugs
in mason jars
by the same people
who taught me
that letting go
meant loving.
Ironic.

In my darkest moments,
I had to learn how to see—
to trace the outline of hope
with trembling hands,
to trust my breath
when nothing else was steady.

I learned to read the quiet,
to listen for myself
beneath the noise of fear,
to find meaning
in the smallest flicker
that refused to go out.

But in my lightest moments,
everyone offered a light—
candles, lanterns, borrowed suns,
hands raised as if
I might forget how bright I was.

They gathered around the glow,
eager to illuminate what was already shining,
to guide me through a room
I could finally see on my own.

Funny how it works—
in the dark,
we teach ourselves vision.
In the light,
the world rushes in
to help us shine

I look in the mirror
and see you in the reflection—
in my early grays,
in the slope of my nose.
I search myself,
hoping you are only surface-deep,
a borrowed shape,
a passing resemblance.
Because if you live deeper than skin,
if you've settled into my bones,
into the way I love or leave—
then I am doomed.

Bury my body in the Camuy sand,
where my soul lives
between those two benches—
never the same,
never okay,
but always there.

Mother Nature cannot fix
what you set ablaze,
but she nurtures
a stable place
for me to lay my feet.
Broken
and miserable,
I stand—
held by the earth
when nothing else would hold me.

I hear the ocean calling—
begging to wrap its waves
around my heart.
It sings in long, aching breaths,
songs of happier souls,
of people who learned
how to let the tide carry them
instead of fighting the pull.
The water remembers things
I am trying to forget,
yet still it calls me home,
salt-soft and relentless,
promising rest
without asking for explanations.
If I step close enough,
it would hold my sorrow gently,
rock it back and forth
until even my grief
learns the rhythm of release.

I stand here anyway,
bare-handed,
asking the light
questions it cannot answer,
hoping that wanting
is the first spark.

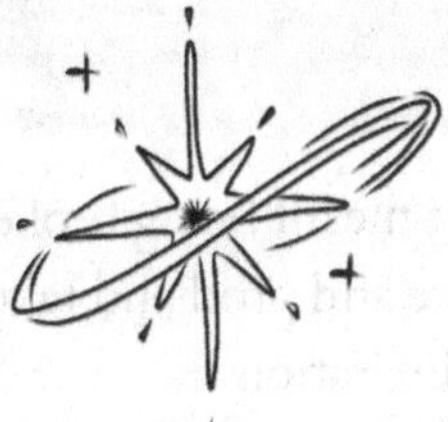

NEBULA

I used to think being soft meant being broken—
meant people would poke and prod and take,
as if tenderness were an invitation
to be worn down.

But now,
I see how strong it is
to stay tender
when the world tells you to harden.
How much courage it takes
to cry in front of someone
and still reach for their hand.

Vulnerability isn't weakness.
It's the way we let the light in,
the quiet whisper of *I'm still here*
even when everything hurts.
There is power
in being a soft place to land.
And today,
I offer that—
to you,
and to myself,
repeatedly.

But even in this hush,
something hums in my bones:
your life is meant to bear fruit.
Not just in flesh,
but in fire,
in thought,
in spirit.

I am fallow ground, and even that has purpose.
I won't rush to bloom.
Today, I will breathe like watering the air.
I will feed myself with quiet, with warmth,
with the stillness of survival.
And when I am ready,
I will grow again-not for anyone else,
not for repair,
but because this life is mine,
and I am worth the harvest.

Stars in the night sky remind me why.
Why my lips taste like hope,
and my heart beats with freedom.
Why the ache in my chest is also a drum,
calling me forward.
Why the wounds I carry glimmer like constellations—
traced by light,
not erased.
Why even in silence,
I am whole,
and even in falling, I rise.
The sky doesn't ask me to be perfect.
It only asks me to keep looking up.

I collect stars like scars,
often and in places I least expect it.
They press against my skin,
burning softly,
reminding me of what I've survived
and what I'm still becoming.
Each one a light I carry
through the dark,
a constellation stitched from memory
and quiet strength.

The ache in my arms
is not weakness—
it is the imprint
of carrying too much.
The ache in my soul
is not a void—
it is the beginning,
clearing space
for something truer.
I remind myself, softly:
I am not nothing.
I am not lost.

I pluck the dreams I once let fade
and plant them in the soil of the moon,
tucking each one into silver dust,
whispering: grow, shine, become.
They drift in quiet orbit,
bathing in starlight,
learning to bloom where the night is wide,
stretching toward constellations
I cannot yet imagine.
One day, they will rise—
bright sparks against the dark,
and I will watch, smiling,
as the dreams I dared to let go
light the sky
with their own gentle fire.

I have awaited this moment of growth for so long,
and now I celebrate myself—
for the strength I have carried,
for surviving through so much of my existence.
At last, I dare to hope
that now is my time to thrive,
to bloom fully, freely,
to reach for light
I once thought out of reach.

My scars have faded—
a quiet sign of renewal,
of becoming.
For if they have been allowed to heal,
it means I, too, have had my chance,
and have changed along with them.

Two girls,
woven together for a lifetime,
threads crossing, tangling,
yet always apart.
One choice
pulled us into different corners of the world,
different shapes of ourselves,
different fires to carry.
But here I stand,
rooted in the life I have claimed,
and I hold only hope
that you, too, have found
a corner of light to call your own.

I crave the gentle recklessness of growth,
of life returning
to every corner
I thought winter had claimed.

We began as sisters,
bound by blood and shared beginnings.
Now we stand apart,
and silence is the only bridge between us.
Let us end that way too—
not in anger, not in forgetting,
but in the quiet understanding
that some bonds are honored
even when left unspoken.

I am out with buckets,
collecting stars.
Only this time,
the night sky does not swallow me whole.
Instead, it gives—
little pockets of purpose,
tiny lights I can hold,
keeping me alive,
reminding me I am enough
to carry my own constellations.

How lucky am I to know a love like my own.

Forgetting you was the dream.
Surviving you was the mission.
Now I'm just forgiving you—
because what cold world does it take
to do what you did to me?

I dance in my kitchen,
inner child's toes twitching like sparks
of a long-forgotten star.
I whisper, "We're safe,"
and the air ignites—
a combustible joy,
freedom blooming
in the quiet corners of my body,
where I have carried wonder
through years of shadows.

The orchid of my past blooms each year,
petals unfolding like tiny planets.
This time, I hold the shears—
pruning carefully,
without mercy,
without fear,
letting only what serves my light remain.

I've built a home on the moon,
in a crater so deep
its jagged edges embrace me.
Here, the stars lean close,
and the universe hums through the silence,
cradling every fragment of me
I thought died.

I was heard without raising my voice,
seen without tearing myself open.
I poured gentleness into myself,
a quiet revolution from my own hands.

Today, I apologize to myself,
for standing in my own way
when all I wanted
was to run toward better spaces,
to breathe freer air,
to let light in without hesitation.

I water my plants,
letting the soil drink deeply.
I water myself too,
each drop a quiet promise.

I am stained glass in an ordinary home—
all color and complexity.
Once, I would have shattered myself to belong.
Now, I stand intact,
catching the light
and shining in my own honor.

If you show me your scars,
I'll hold them like flower petals—
delicate, weathered,
still beautiful.
I won't ask you to explain.
I'll just listen,
quiet and full of breath,
the way the earth listens
after rain.

I know what it is
to fear being too much
or not enough.
I know the flinch
when love comes close—
how sometimes it doesn't stay.
But you stayed.
And that undid something in me,
gently.

If I show you mine,
it won't be loud.
It will be a late-night whisper,
a trembling hand reaching out,
soft stories sewn into my skin.

They aren't always pretty.
Some are tender.
But I'll show you anyway.
Because something about you
feels like a safe place to land—
like warmth in the dark,
like home.

I want the buzzing of bees
to fill my bones,
and the butterflies to
guide my eyes.
I want the grass to ground me,
damp against my feet.

I never felt like enough,
stacked against
the number of other bodies
in my childhood.
Never the chosen one
in the room.
Until I learned
I could make my own magic—
and the rooms grew smaller,
the bodies fewer,
and the kindness
finally meant something.

The bristles of my paintbrush
trace the edges of my life,
blessing them
with celestial color.
As if whimsy
was never forbidden at all.

My dreams are often haunted
by men from my past—
shadows that linger
in the corners of my sleep,
voices that whisper
like wind through empty halls.
I wake with the weight
of their echoes still pressing
against my chest,
a familiar ache.

But the morning is different now.
Sunlight brushes my skin,
and I feel the tremor of my own power,
slow and steady
as it rises from the bones
they once tried to claim.
A smile creeps in,
quiet at first,
then bold, unstoppable,
because I remember
I am not theirs to haunt.

I am mine.
I hold the space they never could,
and even as their memory lingers,
it bends to my strength.
Morning becomes an anthem,
my own heart's drum,
reminding me
that the power I feared losing
was waiting
inside me all along.

I once wrote to survive,
each sentence a hum in the quiet of my own chaos.
Now I write to reach others,
offering a sanctuary
of ink and thought
for those still seeking a way through.

I owe myself a letter of devotion,
filled with quiet nooks and tender syllables.
In the glass, I recognize someone
who once longed for refuge
and received only fractures.
I owe her affirmation,
a gentle haven carved from survival,
a place to exhale without fear.
Here, I will whisper:
you are treasured,
you are whole,
you are finally unharmed within your own presence.

I don't drink coffee,
yet its scent still finds me,
a quiet summons of you.
I no longer let that memory
startle my body.
Instead, I make room
for the version of myself
who endured those mornings,
who learned how to wake
with ache already present.
I honor her now,
not with fear,
but with patience,
allowing the past to pass through
without asking it to stay.

Too many stories revolve
around a man rescuing a woman.
So, I wrote my own,
about a woman lifting herself from the ruins,
stitching courage into her bones.
In her rising,
she illuminates the path
for every woman who will follow,
teaching them how to save themselves,
too.

I watch my son
and see orbits and comets in his gaze,
fragments of light spinning in quiet wonder.
When he calls for me,
each syllable waters the dreams
I buried deep in the soil of myself.
Through him,
the hopes I once planted
awaken and stretch toward the sky.

I am building a home
he will never have to repair.
Every wall, every corner,
a shelter for his heart—
whole, safe, unshaken.

My soul pulses with fresh energy,
rising like fire through the stars,
born within the luminous nebula
of this life I am finally claiming.

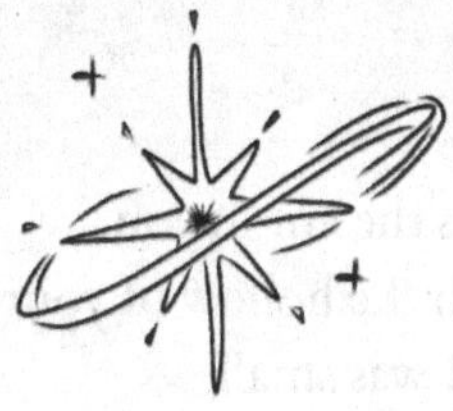

NOVA

The wolf in me swallows the ant in you,
my howl tearing through the hollow of your existence.
For too long, I believed I was small,
measured, broken, meant to bend.

But as I rise, fierce and untamed,
I see it clearly at last.
You are only a man.
No match for the force I have become
from the fire you created.

I am the bug collector,
wandering the terrain of myself
with quiet precision,
as if every crack in my shell
might hide something worth saving.

I kneel in the places I've abandoned,
brush dust from the soft-bodied truths
I buried long ago,
lift my molted layers
like relics, not refuse.

The fragments I couldn't carry—
my sting, my silence,
the way I twitch when light touches a wound—
I gather them all,
patient as dusk, never flinching.

I tuck them gently
into the folds of my memory
like rare wings pressed between pages,
not to possess but to preserve.
With me, I am not dissected;
I am studied, marveled at,
made whole in the slow unfolding
of my many selves.

And maybe that is what love is:
someone who sees the swarm
and doesn't run.
Someone who stays,
and watches,
and whispers that even the things
that buzz and bite
still belong.

Silence scared me
for a long time.
But now I know:
silence is not absence,
not emptiness,
it is an answer.
Sometimes, the only one
worth listening to.

I never thought I'd make it
to where I am now—
lying awake, hoping death
would be as sweet
as falling asleep.
But now I am planting dreams
for years to come.
And instead of counting sheep,
I count my successes,
because they are fruitful,
because they stayed.
How lucky am I
to say I did it—
even alone.
I did it.

Ivy tangles her vines around my legs,
offering her roots for stability,
or at least that is how I always saw it—
a gift, a support, something I could lean on.
But now I see clearly:
the ivy needs me.
It twists and stretches only because I am here,
my strength, my presence,
my willingness to hold it.
It grows because I give it space,
because I anchor it without knowing
that anchoring was never just for me.

I am the ground it claims.
I am the sun it reaches for.
I am the quiet force it bends toward.
And in that, I recognize:
this isn't about ivy.
This is about me.
The roots I thought I supported,
the vines I thought I held,
were reflections of my own power—
my own resilience, my own capacity to nurture
and to be unshakable.

I am not merely a resting place.
I am the storm, the soil, the sky,
and the ivy grows because I choose to grow.
And if I choose to let go,
it will either fall or stretch toward another—
but I will remain,
solid, alive,
unapologetically mine.
This isn't about ivy.
This is about claiming the gravity of myself,
and realizing for the first time
that the world, the people, the green that clings—
all of it—needs me as much as I once thought I needed it.

There are parts of me
that still hold pieces of you.
Fragments, echoes, shadows
that once threatened to consume me—
and yes, at times, they still feel doomed,
like jagged glass pressed against my ribs.
But now, I do not fight them.
I do not shove them into corners,
do not pretend they do not exist.
I work with them.
I let them breathe.
I let them sit on my window sill
where sunlight can touch them,
where they can be seen,
not hidden, not shamed.

The parts of you
that linger within me
have a place here—
a controlled, safe space
where memory is tempered by wisdom,
where hurt is held
but never allowed to strike again.
Because the difference between us
is that I have chosen differently.
I will not use these pieces
to wound another.
I will not weaponize them.
Not ever again.

Instead, I let them teach me.
I let them remind me
of the fragility of human hearts,
the danger of unchecked anger,
the depth of the love I can carry
even after it has been broken.
And in this, I am both vessel and sanctuary.
I hold what once haunted me,
and I transform it—
not into vengeance, not into fear,
but into light.
Into lessons.
Into tenderness.
Into the quiet knowing
that what I carry is mine,
but how I wield it is sacred.

There are parts of you in me, yes.
But they are no longer chains.
They are threads of understanding,
woven into the tapestry of who I am,
visible only because I am strong enough
to let them see the sun—
without letting them burn anyone else.
And that, finally,
is the freedom I have fought for.

Love can be a lantern,
not a weapon.
It can be warmth,
not fire that consumes.
It can be quiet,
not chaos.
And this gentleness,
this stillness,
is a fire too—
a steady flame that does not demand,
does not punish,
does not scorch.

I am learning
that the most radical act
is to protect myself
with tenderness.
That the fiercest revolution
can bloom from softness.
That after a lifetime
of surviving, of burning,
all the body truly wants
is gentleness.

And so, I give it to myself,
every day, every breath,
allowing my fire to illuminate
the spaces where I am gentle,
where I am alive,
where I am wholly
me.

I love you.
I have always loved you.
But love is not a permission slip.
It is not a key to my surrender.
It does not grant the right
to wound me,
to trespass against the life I am building,
to erase the boundaries I have carved
with careful hands and a steady heart.

So, I step back.
I step away.
I claim no contact.
And in that act,
I take back the reigns of my own life,
a simple, terrifying, glorious act
that defines me in ways words cannot hold.

Yes, there will be stories about me.
Stories bent, twisted, designed to fracture my reflection.
Yes, there will be fear,
because the world loves a whisper
and the mind is prone to doubt.
And yes, there will always be people against me—
and sometimes,
sometimes, I will be one of them.
But to be on the side of healing
is to walk a solitary path.
It is to trust your own steps
when the voices howl,
when the light bends through smoke and shadow,
when the ground beneath you feels uncertain.

And yet—
you are never truly alone.
Look up.
See the stars.
The cosmos does not judge.
The stars do not whisper cruelty.
They shine because they are alive,
because they have survived
the same flame you carry
in your chest.

No contact is not a punishment.
It is a declaration.
It is the first true spell you cast
to protect yourself,
to honor your soul,
to claim the universe
that lives inside you.

And when you stand alone,
you will see:
the stars are waiting,
the cosmos bends toward you,
and the most sacred love
is the one you give yourself.

And now, in this Nova,
I am my own explosion,
my own cosmic witness,
my own luminous spell.

I have felt many things—
the ache of loss,
the tremor of first love,
the scorch of rage,
the quiet bloom of wonder in the dark.
Each feeling was a star
that I held in my chest,
and poetry became the telescope
through which I saw it,
the constellation I traced
to understand myself,
to summon my own gravity,
to light my own sky.
Poetry does not have to be gentle.
It does not have to be pretty.
It can sting, it can bite,
it can make the body tremble,
it can make the chest ache
with recognition.

Poetry is not a pattern,
not a rhyme, not a neatly folded line.
Poetry is a pulse,
a heartbeat vibrating through the body,
a spell you cast into the air
and it touches something
you did not know you carried.

I breathe life into my home,
filling every corner with warmth,
every shadow with light.
I breathe life into my son,
into his laughter, his wonder,
the small, fierce spark
that makes him who he is.
I breathe life into my surroundings,
into the objects I touch,
the spaces I move through,
the air itself.
And most of all,
I breathe life into myself—
claiming my body, my mind,
my soul as its own universe,
alive, unbound,
utterly present.

Within me burns a thousand galaxies,
each touch a quiet act of healing.

When I was little,
I knew immediately
that my favorite color was turquoise.
Bright as the shallow sea,
soft as morning light
slipping across a quiet room.
But I never bought turquoise things.
I never told anyone.
I tucked the truth away
like a fragile feather
I feared would be stolen
or laughed at
if I let it breathe in the world.
As an adult, I did the same.
I whispered to myself
that it didn't matter,
that I had other priorities,
that love for a color
was too simple, too small
to claim as my own.
But turquoise kept following me.
In the corner of a shop,
glinting on a keychain,
in the sky after a storm,
on a plate I didn't buy,
on a ribbon I didn't untie.

It wasn't about the color.
It was about allowing myself
to take up space in the world,
to hold things I loved
without shame or excuse,
without waiting for permission
from anyone—especially me.
And now, when I look around,
turquoise is everywhere.
It greets me in my home,
smiles from a cup,
dances on the edges of my notebooks,
as if to say,
"I see you.
You are here.
You have shifted."
And here is the truth I carry,
the advice I whisper
to my younger self,
to anyone listening:
it is an everyday decision.
To let yourself love what you love,
to claim the color,
the joy,
the small, brilliant things
that make your soul sing.
Turquoise is not just a color.
It is a permission slip,
a lighthouse,
a reminder
that the only approval you need
is your own.

Step forward.
Become the cosmos you were always meant to be.

There is a light at the end of the tunnel.
But it is not given.
It is not waiting for you.
It is a light you must cast yourself,
strike by strike,
moment by moment,
until the darkness bends
and the path ahead becomes visible.

Because the truest light
is the one you create.

In this moment,
I am amongst the stars—
in the vast, quiet brilliance
where I was always meant to be.
No gravity can pull me down.
No shadow can dim my glow.
I have arrived
and I shine,
just as I was born to.

There will come a time
when someone you love
makes a choice that shatters everything.
In that moment,
do not lose yourself.
Remember your fire.
Feel it burn inside you,
steady and undeniable.
Then look at their hands.
Do they reach toward your flame,
to nurture it, to shield it,
or do they try to snuff it out?
Do not give them your heat
if they would douse it.
Do not surrender your light
to someone who cannot hold it.
Your fire is yours—
and it is sacred.

I used to think being chronically ill
was the sentence the universe gave me
for the mistakes of my family.
But now I know:
this body, this pain, this endurance—
it is mine.
No one else could walk this path,
no one else could hold this fire,
no one else could know the strength
that comes from being the friend
who knows pain intimately,
like an old companion
I chose, not inherited.
I carry it fully.
I claim it.
I am not sentenced.
I am forged.

I no longer ache over quiet mouths
that move only for the favored.
I no longer chase the shadowed applause
of those who cheer only
when others have cleared the sky.

There is power in the loud blessing—
in the voices that name your dreams
like spells
that cannot be undone.

The day I knew I healed
was the day I noticed
my hobbies shifted
from hurting myself
to investing in myself.
Because there was a future—
not an impending doom.

I cry rubies.
My tears are valuable.
I no longer shed them without intention.
For years, I gave rubies
to things that deserved far less—
if not nothing at all.
Now, each drop burns with purpose,
each fall a testament
to the love I save for what matters.

I am a little girl,
white curtains swaying
in the spring air.
Your radio playing tunes.
It is the only memory
I have not stained with tears.
I hold on to it—
but not on to you.

They thought nova meant large.
Flames growing.
Heat rising.
Anger boiling.
Revenge.
Instead, it meant
collapse into light—
a final giving,
not an explosion of hate
but a release so bright
it remade everything around it.

I will never be okay
with what you did to me.
But I will spend every second
making sure I no longer carry
the blame
for your lack of love.

My dreams are now sprouted,
a patchwork of me
scattered across the Moon.
Cratered hopes,
soft-lit wishes,
pieces of myself learning
how to grow in low gravity.

And every night,
I tend to them—
watering what once felt impossible,
trusting that even here,
in borrowed light,
I am allowed to bloom.

In my bedroom, there's a wall
full of flowers.
Each one, I imagine,
is a past version of myself.
Some battered.
Some blue.
I invite them all over,
sit with them in the quiet,
and thank each version of me
for getting me through.

My bones are made of carnelian,
crafted in heat, with time.
Iron-stained and slow-formed,
pressed into color by everything
that tried to break me open.

I was not forged in spectacle,
no sudden blaze, no rebirth myth—
just quiet exposure,
years of warmth and waiting,
pressure learning my name.

What lives beneath my skin now
is not survival,
but saturation—
a deep, earned red
that remembers every flame
and chose to stay.

Fire did not consume me.
It settled into my marrow,
taught me how to glow
without burning myself alive.

I am not a phoenix rising from the ashes.
I am a moth following a light—
only this light is my own,
forged from a fire within.
And damn it,
it is beautiful.

I have found my fire.
It courses through my veins,
a sweetness potent enough
to bring unhealed souls
to their knees.
My corner is no longer
a dwelling of what I survived,
but a shrine to all
I have given life to.
I have found my fire,
and in it—
my sweet release.

ABOUT THE AUTHOR

Hailey Renee crafts cozy romance and poetry rooted in representation, heartfelt connection, and the subtle magic of everyday life.

Beyond writing, Hailey supports fellow authors as a personal assistant, crafts beauty as a florist, and embraces tradition as a folk practitioner. Whether through words, blooms, or a touch of old-world wisdom, she believes in the power of storytelling to heal, to connect, and to bring a little more love into the world.

ALSO BY HAILEY RENEE

The Homegrown Hearts Collection:

Beyond the Teacups

Where Wildflowers Bloom

The Caneberry Trilogy

A Patchwork of Us

www.ingramcontent.com/pod-product-compliance
Lightning Source LLC
Chambersburg PA
CBHW021809130726
47987CB00010B/3078